The Go Seek Map

by Holly Harper

illustrated by Isabel Muñoz

OXFORD
UNIVERSITY PRESS

Aisha has a sheet. It contains the Go Seek Map.

Go seek this!
It has a tail
and feet.

A goat has a tail.
But it has no feet.

She has a
tail and feet.

Aisha and Kadeena roam the bank.

Peek in the reeds.
A boatman!

Can we see a queen?
Eek! It is a bee!

Aisha wails.

Go seek this! It feeds on oats.
A foal?

Lightning and rain!

Kadeena tugs on her coat.

Aisha moans.

We might not see a foal.
Seek Map

We did not finish the Go Seek Map.
Wait! See Beth?

OATS
We can feed oats to her!
We did it!
Go Seek Map

Look Back

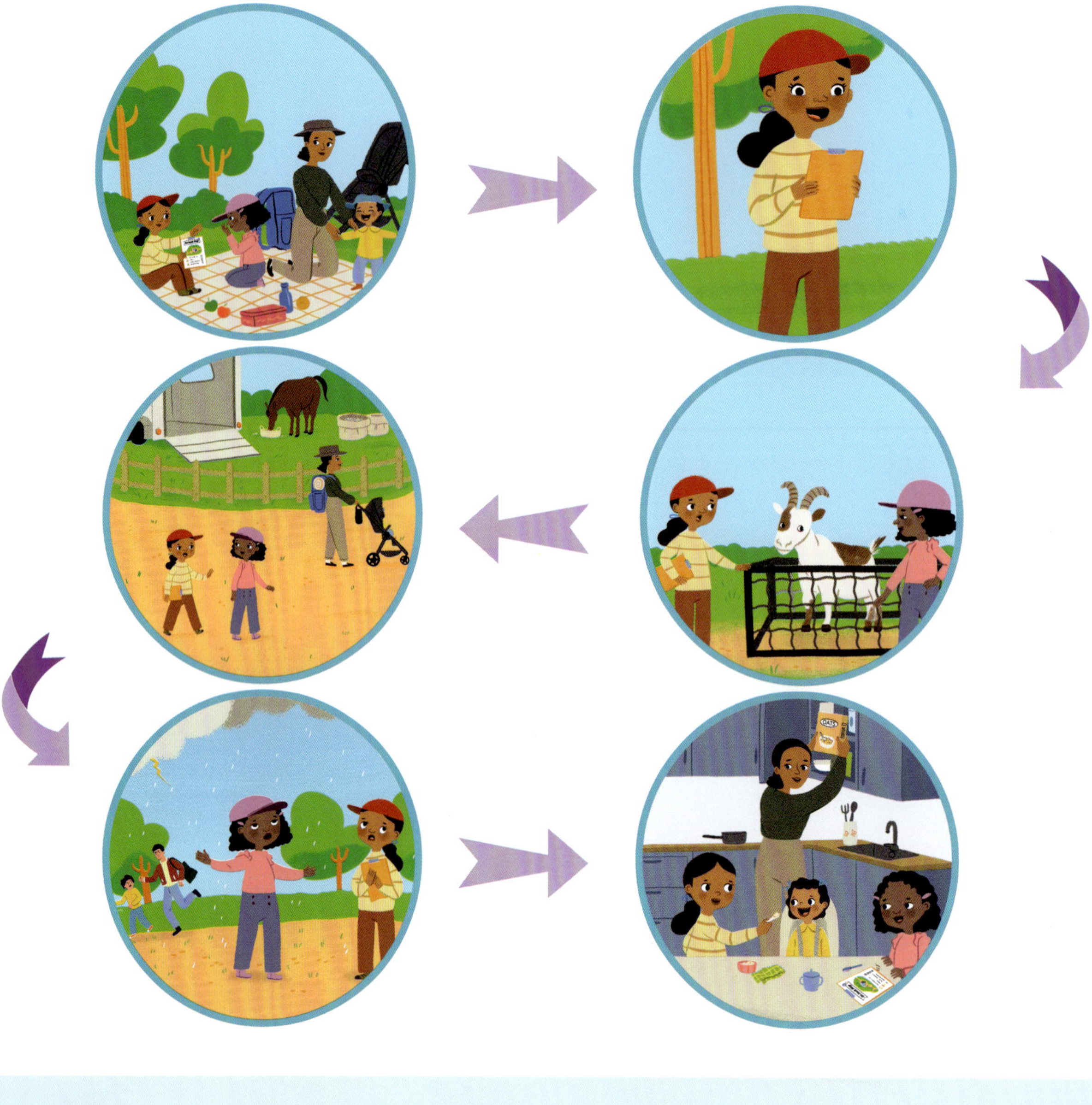

Encourage students to use the pictures to retell the story.